# THEN &

# SHEFFIELD

## Broomhill, Crookes, Fulwood, Crosspool, Lodge Moor, Nether Green

### ald
Print

## Alistair Lofthouse

# Acknowledgements

My thanks go to:

Alison Swift for assisting in research.

Sheffield Local studies Library, Surrey Street, who have provided many of the pictures in this book. All images shown with a reference number at the bottom right are on their website: **www.picturesheffield.co.uk**

Copies of pictures may be ordered online.

© Alistair Lofthouse 2008

Printed and published by:
ALD Design & Print
279 Sharrow Vale Road
Sheffield  S11 8ZF

Telephone  0114 267 9402
E:mail  a.lofthouse@btinternet.com

ISBN 9-781-901587-76-0

First Published September 2008

**You can view/order our entire range of books through our secure on-line ordering system on:**

## www.printanddesignshop.co.uk

# Introduction

*Then & Now Sheffield S10* continues our successful *Then & Now* series which so far covers *Sheffield Central, The Blitz, Sheffield 11 and Sheffield 6*.

Although lacking much industry with S10 being a largely residential area, this book does show the contrast of areas with great change against areas of little change, for example the ongoing development of Sheffield University from 1905 is very evident.

Included are brief histories of some of the most influential people who have lived in the area and whose donations to the city are still around today. The area is also famed for its Victorian buildings that were described in the following passage:

*"I thought of the leafy district of Broomhill on the western heights of Sheffield, where gabled black stone houses rise above the ponticums and holly, and private cast-iron lamp-posts light the gravelled drives. Greek, Italian, Gothic, they stand in winding tree-shaded roads, these handsome mansions of the Victorian industrialists who made their pile from steel and cutlery in the crowded mills below. They lived in what is still the prettiest suburb in England."*

*Extract from: John Betjeman, Telegraph and Morning Post, July 3 1961.*

Much of Broomhill grew up around the Sheffield to Manchester Turnpike that opened in the 1920s. There is also talk of a racecourse being at what is now Broomhill in the 18th Century. To go further back the Roman road from Templebrorough to Navio (Brough) passed through much of S10 although much of the route is unknown but one guess is that it went up Brook Hill and then across to Lodge Moor.

Although I have mainly lived in S11 I did for a few years in the mid 1970s live in S10 at Burnt Stones Drive, Sandygate Park. I recall long hot, dry summers, cold winters with a few feet of snow and the visits of the cream and red Fletcher's bread and cake vans - all now gone!


Alistair Lofthouse

August 2008

Lodge Moor Hospital, opened in 1888 closed in 1995. Once an isolation hospital, hence its somewhat isolated position. The last iron lung was still here in the 1970s. Situated on Redmires Road near to the old Roman Road which runs from Templeborough, Rotherham to Brough-on-Noe, Bradwell. Now a housing estate.

Another view of Lodge Moor 'Fever' Hospital at Redmires. Opened in response to a small pox epidemic. Smallpox killed around 30% of the infected but the disease was eradicated by 1980. In December 1955 a US Air Force F-84 Thunderstrike jet crashed into the building killing one woman.

Crimicar Lane Hospital & Sanatorium. Opened in November 1902 and closed in May 1956. It was used as a general isolation unit. Prior to the First World War the hospital was primarily used to treat cases of smallpox, but consumptive (tuberculosis) patients were admitted if smallpox cases were lacking. Many patients were those associated with the cutlery industry where grindstones and buffing wheels created a huge amount of gritty dust. Silicosis was the cause of great mortality, as was tuberculosis which was often associated with the 'dolly polishing' of silverware. The hospital buildings were later demolished to make way for housing and all that remains are part of the perimeter wall and gates.

Brookhouse Hill. This road ran down to the River Porter and got its name from a 17th Century house that was located close to the brook.

Willow Croft, home for the elderly on Fulwood Road was replaced with new housing in the late 1990s. A new road, Fulwood Chase was created.

TRAM TERMINUS,
NETHER GREEN.

Nether Green Tram Terminus joined the tram routes from Broomhill and Hunter's Bar. The Broomhill branch along Fulwood Road was one of the first to close in August 1936. The tall building in the background is Ranmoor United Methodist College. Storth Lane joining in the middle of the picture was originally called Water Lane. On the east side of Storth Lane stood the Rand Moor Cutlery Works of J & J Beal who were scissorsmiths, the water for the grinding wheels coming from one of the springs on the steep hillside.

Nether Green Tram Terminus.    The Nether Green to Hunter's Bar tram route closed in 1952.  The old house was converted into flats in the 2000s and the motor car now clearly dominates this scene.

Closer view of the Ranmoor United Methodist College, Fulwood Road, used for the training of ministers for the Methodist New Connection which had split from the Wesleyans. Thomas Firth bequeathed £5,000 towards the building which was opened in 1864 by his son Mark.

Oakbrook Road, Nether Green. The Council once planned a roundabout at the junction of Hangingwater Road and Oakbrook Road. A strip of land, off to the left of the photograph on Nethergreen Road was purchased to allow road widening, but the plans never went ahead.

Ranmoor. The Bulls Head pub on the left hand side was originally called the Highland Laddie.

Fulwood Road, Ranmoor. This row of shops was built to supply the expanding population of Ranmoor over one hundred years ago and remains remarkably unaltered today. Note the intricate detail on the pole that holds the tram wires.

Oakbrook House now Notre Dame School. Designed by William Flockton and built in 1860 for Mark Firth. In 1875 the Prince and Princess of Wales came to Sheffield and stayed at Oakbrook House. The house was owned by the Laycock family of engineering fame 1884 to 1919 when it was then purchased by Notre Dame convent for £15,000. Oakbrook is now the school's 6th form block.

*Mark Firth 1819-1880*

Mark Firth was born in Sheffield on the 25th April 1819. His father, Thomas, was Head Melter at the Crucible Steel Works of Sanderson Brothers. The family was large, Mark having six brothers and three sisters.

Mark and his brother Thomas junior started in work at Sanderson Brothers but soon left to set up their own business in Charlotte Street, Sheffield in 1842. Thomas senior joined them shortly afterwards. Thomas Firth & Sons was thus formed. Together with his father, Mark Firth built up a steel works and he became a very rich man and a major public figure.

The firm started slowly but by 1852, business was so good that they had to move to larger premises at the Norfolk Works, in Saville Street. The works had crucible furnaces, a file making shop and the largest rolling mill in Sheffield. Two Nasmyth Steam forge hammers were installed to allow Firth's to develop their business into the armaments market. The hammers were used to forge guns. Two larger steam hammers were installed in 1863. The noise and vibration of these hammers caused the neighbouring businesses to complain that their machinery was being damaged. In 1871, Firth's cast the thirty five ton Woolwich Infant gun. In 1875, they produced an eighty ton gun. At this stage, Firth's were employing over a thousand workers.

Mark Firth was at this stage, one of the wealthiest people in Sheffield. He was elected Mayor of Sheffield in 1874, and achieved the great honor of Master Cutler when he was elected to the office in 1867. He was re-elected for the following two years.

In 1875 he built a mansion for himself at Oakbrook, Ranmoor on the outskirts of the town, designed by William Flockton in 1860, and he had the 26 ½ acres surrounding it laid out as his garden. Gas and water were brought to the locality when he moved there.

In 1875 Mark Firth entertained the then Prince and Princess of Wales - later King Edward VII & Queen Alexandra at Oakbrook during his year as Mayor. Grand as Oakbrook was, Firth decided it was not grand enough and had it extended and improved, with the addition of a stone porch. A dinner for the Prince and Princess was given and guests included the Archbishop of York, the Duke of Norfolk, the Earl and Countess Fitzwilliam, Lord John and Lady Manners and Sir John Brown.

His house, which eventually passed out of private hands, was later bought by William S Laycock who moved across the road from his former home at 'Rosemount' 404 Fulwood Road. Laycock had invented a patent railway carriage blind which helped to make his fortune. It is now Notre Dame School.

Shortly after Firth moved there John Brown (1816-96) bought the old Endcliffe Hall in 1863 and had it completely re-built. In 1864 Mark Firth and John Brown along with other leading silversmiths took part in an emergency meeting to set up and find urgent relief for the sufferers of the Sheffield Flood.

By 1885 it was said of him that *other manufacturers, merchants and professional men followed his lead moving to the outskirts of the city and now there is scarcely an eligible site upon which is not a fine residence standing in extensive grounds, and encircled by the mingled works of nature and art.*

In 1875, Mark bought a thirty-six acre estate which he presented to the town of Sheffield as Firth Park.

Mark was the founder of Firth College, which later became the University of Sheffield.

Following his death in 1880 a monument was erected in the General Cemetery, the decorative ironwork being forged in his own works. His monument is one of the grandest in the cemetery and remains a physical reminder of Sheffield's supremacy in the Victorian steel industry.

*Mark Firth's Grave today*

S01342

Ringstead Crescent, Crosspool. The house, which belonged to the Haywood family, was destroyed during the air raid on 13th December 1940.

Crosspool. Most of the houses in the above scene still exist today, but now as retail properties. This picture is taken from Watt Lane which runs into Sandygate Road.

Looking up Sandygate Road from Manchester Road. Henry Bradbury the Grocer & Sub-Postmaster occupied Nos 2-6 Sandygate Road (on the corner).

Manchester Road, Crosspool. For many years there was a petrol station on the right. To the left is the original Crosspool Tavern. As the name suggests, this road was the main turnpike road from Sheffield to Manchester which opened in the 1820s.

S00475

Manchester Road, Crosspool. The Crosspool Tavern has been totally rebuilt and moved further back from the road, possibly to allow for road widening.

Lydgate Hall in Dereliction. Now occupied by Lydgate Hall Crescent. Horatio Bright lived at Lydgate Hall from 1881 - 1906. He was a prominent business partner of the steel manufacturing firm Turton, Bright & Co., who made quality dies for the Royal Mint. After his death in 1906 the hall stood empty for twenty years before becoming a boarding house. It was then used by the Conservatives for their 'Young Conservative' meetings before being demolished in 1950s.

John Bly's blacksmith shop, Lydgate Lane, with Mount Zion in the background, which was also known as Wesley Tower. Most of Bly's business appears to be cartwheel repairs. ALD, the publishers of this book are based in similar ex smithy buildings on Sharrow Vale Road.

S06238

Cottages on Tapton Hill Road, near Lydgate Lane junction, replaced in 1940 by a housing scheme founded by J. G. Graves.

Tapton Hill Congregational Church built in 1913 by Chapman, Jenkin & Son. Later additions have included a new entrance porch, mini bell tower and church hall to the left.

Fulwood Road. The gatehouse still stands though double yellow lines now replace the tram lines. The Hallam Towers Hotel was opened in 1965 in time for use in the 1966 World Cup. Recently closed, plans are that this iconic building should become apartments.

Tapton Court was presented to the Royal Hospital for use as nurse's home in 1934 by J. G. Graves. A new wing, in the background, was built just before World War II. Sheffield University now uses the site but the old house is unused in 2008.

Fulwood Road looking towards Broomhill - to the left out of view was the old Sheffield blind school. Situated a conservation area Broomhill has retained its tree-lined streets.

Manchester Road. Still the bus route from Broomhill to Lodge Moor. The above picture shows a motorbus as no tram lines were laid on this route.

Fulwood Road and Manchester Road. The tram shown is No. 86 and is part of a batch of 200 built between 1918 and 1927 and seated 76 people. They were known as enclosed cars as the earlier design had partially open top decks and which were open at either end.

The original church steeple was hit by lightening in the 1970s and was then removed and, shortly after, the church was demolished. The site remained empty until the 1990s when the new church was built on the site.

Fulwood Road, Broomhill - the shops still remain today although the road has been widened. The Shopping Centre was the one of the best and reached its peak during the Second World War when several stores and shops that had been bombed out in the city relocated to Broomhill. The foremost being John Walsh Ltd which moved into The Mount follow the destruction of their High Street shop.

The above sign is situated above the shops and shows that the shops here used to be known as a market.

Fulwood Road. Thos. W. Ward a familiar Sheffield name had a coal merchants shop here, note how the two small shops are now just one.

The original enamel Fulwood Road sign still remains today and can be seen to the right of the drainpipe.

Fulwood Road/Glossop Road. The Carsick Hill Land Society, established in 1876, were building speculators attracted to the area by 'big names' of the day moving into the area. They had regular meetings at the York Hotel. The names have changed over the years more recently being O'Neil's Irish Bar but finally reverted back to the York recently under the Scream brand. It is now popular with students.

Crookes Road/Whitham Road. The buildings to the left were built in the early 1970s replacing a Victorian row of buildings. This would not be allowed today!

S20550

Fulwood Road, this view virtually unchanged today. Note the later style plain trampole, as opposed to those shown on the previous few pages. Many remained until the late 1970s as lamp posts, although the trams had long since gone. They were all painted green.

Whitham Road, named and built in the 1860s. This picture is taken from infront of Westbourne House which is now Weston Park hospital.

To the left was Godfrey Dam which is now the University of Sheffield sports pitches.

Ashdell Road, said to be named after Ashdell Grange which was built in the early 1800s. The Grange had large gardens, said to be laid out by Joseph Paxton. I wonder who the girl was and is that a hat or parasol?

Girls High School opened in 1878 with 39 pupils on a site in Surrey Street, Sheffield. It moved to this site in 1887 and now has many more pupils and has much expanded over the years. In recent times there have been link ups with nearby Birkdale Boys School in order to share facilities.

Botanical Gardens. The covered passages that joined these three Victorian conservatories were removed in 1906. The gardens have recently been restored to their former glory. A 1999 picture, inset left, shows them before restoration. The pavilions are grade II listed.

The Botanical Gardens were opened in 1836 and designed by Robert Marnock. The bandstand has long since gone. The recent restoration of the gardens spanning some 6 years has cost more than £5 million, with funding coming through Heritage Lottery and public support.

Weston Park was built in 1910 and was also designed by Robert Marnock. Originally a private house for the Harrison Family it was opened in 1871 as a museum. The Mappin art gallery was added later. The museum suffered extensive bomb damage in 1940. In 2001 through heritage lottery funding a rebuild commenced, reopening in 2006. In 1882 a weather station was created here and still operates today.

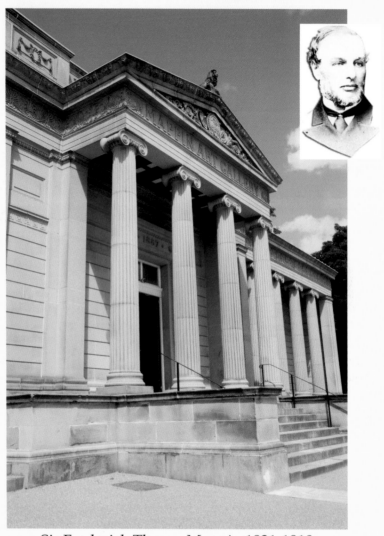

Sir Frederick Thorpe Mappin 1821-1910

Often referred to the father of Sheffield University, donating £9000 towards its building, Mappin was the first Chancellor of the University in 1905. Cutlery was Mappin's business, initially as manager of the family business, Mappin Brothers, and then partner at Thomas Turton.

He was Master Cutler in 1855 and Lord Mayor in 1877. After the death of his uncle John Mappin in 1884 Frederick oversaw the completion of the Mappin Art Gallery and also gave eighty of his own paintings for the permanent collection.

Sheffield Children's Hospital was opened in 1903 in the building that has since been extended several times to accommodate the work that now takes place in children's care. There are approximately 140 acute beds in the Children's Hospital and there is also a 20 place Day Case Unit for day surgery.

Sheffield Children's Hospital. The building in the background was J.G. Graves' warehouse on a site now occupied by the Octagon Centre which opened in 1983. The Octagon Centre provides Sheffield University with exhibition and conference facilities and is also a concert venue.

Y01249

Sheffield University's Firth Court on the left was opened in 1905. J.G. Graves' building on the right where the Octagon now stands. The dual carriageway overpass was built in the late 1960s.

S22443

Durham Road. J.G. Graves donated the land to Sheffield university and the student union opened on this site in 1936. Note the ornate company logo in the brickwork in the end of the wall (above).

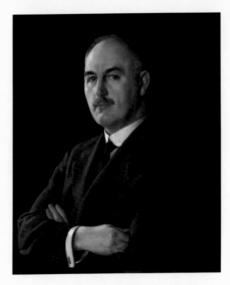

J. G. Graves 1866 -1945

There are a fair few places in Sheffield bearing the name Graves; Graves Park, Graves Art Gallery and many housing schemes around the city.

All of these are due to John George Graves, a successful local businessman who donated over £1millon during his life to Sheffield. Graves was not actually from Sheffield but came to the city from Lincolnshire to become an apprentice watchmaker.

He established one of the countries first mail order companies, initially selling watches but then branching out into a vast array of household goods including toys. In its heyday, with premises where Sheffield University Octagon is now located, he had yearly sales of over £1million and employed around 3,000 people. He was elected Lord Mayor in 1926.

Graves was an enthusiastic art collector and he donated £30,000 to help build the Surrey Street Central library complete with an art gallery on the top floor that bears his name. The Graves Gallery had a policy of having temporary exhibitions alongside permanent displays, an idea established by the galleries first director J. Rothenstein who later went on to become the director of the Tate Gallery.

Ecclesall Woods, Concord Park and Blacka Moor were some of the gifts of land that Graves gave to the city. After his death his business was sold to Great Universal Stores of Manchester who continue to trade under Argos, Marshall Ward, Kays and Littlewoods.

Oakley class lifeboat, built in 1958 that served until 1993 named J.G. Graves of Sheffield. This was the first of this particular class of lifeboat and served for around 20 years at Scarborough. It is now preserved at Chatham Historic Dockyard in the R.N.L.B. exhibition.

Examples of J.G. Graves adverts

321 Glossop Road - The above picture show the Slinn Family who have just taken over from the Turners in 1949. The property is said to have been a chemist shop for around 100 years. Inset with the new name and new modern windows it was run by Mr D W Slinn until 1974 when he died. It then became Scotts Pantry which it has been ever since. Buildings over the road on the left have been replaced by Sheffield University buildings.

Glossop Road commemorative arch, one of seven erected in the city for the Royal Visit of Edward VII and Queen Alexandra on 12th July 1905. The temporary arch was constructed of wood and plaster board. Edward was in Sheffield to open the Firth Court Building of the University of Sheffield on Western Bank. King Edward VII School was founded in 1905 and named after the king.

Upper Hanover Street before becoming part of the Inner Ring Road during the late 1970s. This 1960s picture shows a much quieter scene.

Somme Barracks on Glossop Road, taking its name from the infamous First World War Battle in which 60,000 troops died in a few days. It is now home to Sheffield University Cadet Corp.

Glossop Road - The Tramlines went in 1960 only to come back in 1993. The Sinclair Building was originally opened in the 1960s. It was demolished and rebuilt in 2006 and won the RIBA White Rose award for architecture in 2007.

Lydgate Lane/Crookes junction - The Grindstone pub is all that remains in this scene. The opposite side of the road was damaged by a bomb in the Second World War. The area was re-built in the 1970s. The Old Grindstone is alleged to be situated at the end of a lane which led to several former quarries, the source of grindstones. Over 190 years old it is mentioned in the 1828 chronicle 'The history of Crookes'

Crookes - a busy shopping street - No 13 on the corner is Ashmore's family butchers. Noah's Ark pub is in the distance. The name Crookes is said to come from old Norse *Krokr* meaning corner of land!

Wesley Hall Crookes, opened in 1836 and still used as a church today. It has an unusual eight sided octagonal layout. ELR once occupied part of this building for heir auctions.

Crookes 1906. The road has since been widened. In a strange coincidence of fate in the picture above, T.R. Ball's shoe shop is closing due to expiry of lease, below 102 years later, the estate agents premises have just come up for rent. In summer 2008 it was not just the sky that looked stormy!

Crookes, northern end which, like the southern end, was dominated by small quarries of which there were three around here. A quarry off to the right of the picture was called Dark Lane Quarry with another in the general position of the petrol station, just visible in the middle of the picture below.

Crookes Valley Park. Containing the Old Great Dam and Dam House Restaurant. The houses in the background are still there today but hidden by 100 years of tree growth!

Winter Street Hospital was opened in 1881 for the victims of smallpox and was known as the Borough Hospital for Infectious Diseases. By 1912 patients were transferred to Lodge Moor with Winter Street being used for tuberculosis cases. During the First World War it became a Military Base Hospital and all the TB cases were sent to Crimicar Lane Sanatorium. In 1919 it once again took in TB cases. As new drugs and treatments eradicated TB, the hospital eventually changed use and became known as St Georges, nursing geriatric patients. It is now is the Sheffield University Dept of Law.

# Bibliography

| | | |
|---|---|---|
| Sheffield | Ruth Harman<br>John Minnis | Pevsner |
| Sheffield Blitz | Paul License | Star |
| Street Names Of Sheffield | Peter Harvey | Sheaf |
| Sheffield Public Houses | Michael Liversidge | Pickards |
| Old Ordnance Survey Maps | | Godfrey |

*Road sign, at least 100 years old, now needing some attention!*

These are a few more of our titles you may enjoy

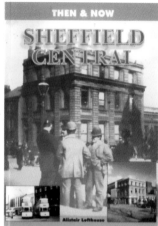

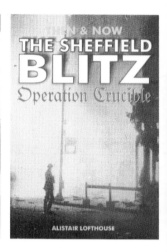

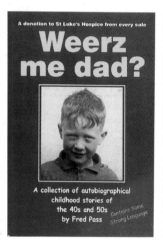

available in all good bookshops or online at:

**www.printanddesignshop.co.uk**